Creative Prayer Activities
Primary Level

created by Elizabeth Wells and Lisa Trout

God's Gifts Reproducible Activity Series
E.T. NEDDER Publishing

Elizabeth Wells is a full-time, free-lance writer and editor who over the past 10 years has written several books and hundreds of articles for both the adult and childrens market. She received a Bachelor of Arts degree in Interdisciplinary Studies from the University of Nebraska at Omaha. The product of Catholic education, she and her husband are active in their three children's schools.

Lisa Trout has been a freelance writer and illustrator for 10 years. Her work has been published in magazines and newspapers across the country. She earned a BA in the Distributed Studies of art, English, and psychology from Iowa State University. She teaches kindergarten Sunday School and is happily married with three wonderful children.

Cover Design: Fun `N Faith, LP
Editor   Kate Harrison

Additional copies of this publication may be produced by sending check or money order for $9.95 plus $3.50 postage and handling to: E.T. NEDDER Publishing, PMB 299, 9121 East Tanque Verde STE 105, Tuscon, Arizona 85749-8930. Or call toll free 1-877-817-2742. Fax: 1-520-760-5883. Email: RINGTAIL@prodigy.net

ISBN 1-893757-06-4

10 9 8 7 6 5 4 3 2

Dear Teacher,

Prayer is one of the most exciting foundations of faith. We are filled with wonder and a sense of connectedness when we pray. And establishing a solid prayer life, especially when young, has life-long faith benefits. The following are some suggestions for making these pages a wondrous experience for you and your students.

You will notice that the beginning of the book is devoted to basic information on prayer. The rest is divided into sections by prayer. The group of prayers and mysteries that make up the Rosary follows this.

The pages can be used to enhance learning of specific prayers, while the general information on prayer can be used at any time you choose to focus on prayer.

Page 5

When you begin discussing prayer in the classroom, ask if anyone knows what a "chat" is. Chances are good that most will have some idea. Help them understand the difference between a "chat" and a speech. Communicate the informality and closeness this involves.

Page 6

Ask the students which gifts they treasure from God. The categories listed on the page are a starting point. Help the students to be as specific as possible in identifying the treasured gifts. The actual collection of items can be done as a class or can be an opportunity for the students' families to become involved.

Page 7

Our world has shortened the distance between peoples with technology. Discuss what technology helps us to connect with others around the world and in space. Expand on why none of that technology is necessary in prayer.

Page 8

This is a great page for discussing how through prayer and actions, we are light in the world.

Pages 9 and 11

Jesus told us that if we ask His heavenly Father in His name, He will give us that for which we are asking. Share this with the students. Also discuss that the answer to prayer is not always the answer we want. Talk about how God knows what is best for us and sometimes we may be asking for things that could harm us in the long run.

Page 10

This project is similar to the treasure hunt activity in that it asks the students to identify the many blessings God gives us. It is important to be specific in naming these because the purpose is to see the abundance of blessings.

Pages 12 - 13

The key to being able to praise God is to be able to recognize the many gifts and blessings He gives. Since the students have been specific in two other activities regarding these gifts and blessings, the cornucopia is more general. The emphasis here is on giving thanks. Discuss how we feel when we are thankful. That feeling of joy easily can be converted to praise, especially to God.

Page 14

If possible, read or have the students read about several saints. (See *Can the Saints Come Out to Play?*, E.T. Nedder Publishing) Use this knowledge to complete the activity.

Pages 15 - 17

Because the Apostles' Creed contains so much information, breaking it into stories is helpful. There is a section on God the Father, Jesus beginning with His birth and ending with His place in heaven. Each of the remaining parts is a statement of either someone or an idea we believe as Catholics. These beliefs are the foundation of our faith. It is what all apostles, us included, say as a continuation of sharing our faith. On page 16, expand the idea of who is the Communion of Saints? What is "saint material?"

Page 18

When the Angel Gabriel visited Mary, she could have easily said no. Develop awareness. What does God ask of each of us? How can we say yes?

Pages 20 - 21

This small prayer's punch is its promise. Help the children see God's constancy and how He promises to be with us forever.

Page 22

The bread can be made at school or at home. In the classroom, focus on daily bread as an umbrella under which all our needs fit. What are our needs?

Page 24

Help the students gain awareness that every day has joy and sufferings. Discuss how can they offer these for grace.

Page 26

Talk about how much better we all feel when we say sorry. Upon completion, either have the students give their card to the person to whom they wrote the note, or present it at the altar during a special reconciliation service.

Page 27

Expand the meaning of grace to include the ability to rise above temptation.

Page 28

Prayer bead activity: You need 12 pony beads and string, 7" long, per student. Ten of the beads should be the same color and the remaining two should be another. Knot one end of the string and then slide one of the two beads onto the string. Make sure your knots are big enough so they don't pull through. Knot and then slide the 10 beads on next. Knot again. String last bead on and tie the final knot. The two beads represent the Our Father and the Glory Be. The 10 represent the Hail Marys.

Page 29

Use the crowns to decorate an existing Mary shrine or to create one in the classroom.

Page 30 - 32

If possible, break into five small groups. Have each group act out a short version of one of the Joyful Mysteries. For the Sorrowful Mysteries, discuss the sacrifices Jesus made so that we might live. What sacrifices can we make each day? Help the students grow in their understanding of the promise of eternal life through the Glorious Mysteries.

Prayer Review Sheet

The Apostles' Creed

I believe in God, the Father Almighty, creator of Heaven and Earth; and in Jesus Christ, His only Son, our Lord; who was conceived of the Holy Spirit, born of the Virgin Mary, suffered under Pontius Pilate, was crucified, died and was buried. He decended into Hell; the third day, He rose from the dead; He ascended into Heaven, and sits at the right hand of God, the Father; He shall come to judge the living and the dead. I believe in the Holy Spirit, the Holy Catholic Church, the Communion of Saints, the forgiveness of sins, the resurrection of the body and life everlasting. Amen.

Our Father

Our Father, who art in Heaven, hallowed be thy name. Thy Kingdom come, Thy will be done on Earth as it is in Heaven. Give us this day, our daily bread, and forgive us our trespasses, as we forgive those who trespass against us. And lead us not into temptation, but deliver us from evil. Amen.

Hail Mary

Hail Mary, full of grace, the Lord is with you. Blessed are you among women and blessed is the fruit of your womb Jesus.

Holy Mary, mother of God, pray for us sinners, now and at the hour of our death. Amen.

Act of Contrition

O my God, I am very sorry for offending you, and I detest all of my sins because they displease you who are all good and deserving of my love. I firmly resolve with the help of your grace to confess my sins, to do penance, and to change my life. Amen.

Hail Holy Queen

Hail Holy Queen, Mother of mercy, our life, our sweetness, and our hope, to you do we cry poor banished children of Eve. To you do we send up our sighs, mourning, and weeping in this valley of tears. Turn then most gracious advocate, your eyes of mercy toward us, and after this our exile, show unto us the blessed fruit of your womb Jesus. O clement, O loving, O sweet Virgin Mary. Pray for us, O Holy Mother of God, that we may be made worthy of the promises of Christ. Amen.

Morning Offering

O Jesus, through the Immaculate Heart of Mary, I offer you all of my prayers, works, joys and sufferings of this day. For all of the intentions of your Sacred Heart, in union with the Holy Sacrifice of the Mass throughout the world, in reparation for my sins, but most of all for the intentions recommended this month by our Holy Father. Amen.

Glory Be

Glory be to the Father, and to the Son, and to the Holy Spirit. As it was in the beginning, is now and ever shall be world without end. Amen.

A Chat with Our Father

God, the Father, hears us whenever we talk to Him. He hears us anywhere we are. That is because He lives within each one of us. Prayer is simply talking to God.

Some prayers are formal. When we pray those prayers, we use the same words that other people all around the world use. This kind of prayer helps us feel close to God and part of the bigger Church.

Some prayers are informal. These prayers are more like a chat with God. It may be to tell Him you love Him or how wonderful something is. It may be to say you need some help. It may be to ask for help for someone else. The words of this prayer simply start in your heart.

Color and cut out the heart. Pin it on your
shirt as a reminder that God is always close by
and you can chat with Him at any time.

Tradition of Prayer

Prayer doesn't just happen. We believe that the Holy Spirit inspires us to pray. The Holy Spirit teaches the children of God to pray and how to hope. The Holy Spirit teaches us to treasure being close to God.

Color and cut out the Paraclete, a symbol for the Holy Spirit. Glue it to the top of a decorated shoebox.

Then go on a treasure hunt. Find things that fit into these groups: creation and nature, God's Word, the sacraments, and Jesus' love. Fill the box with these things.

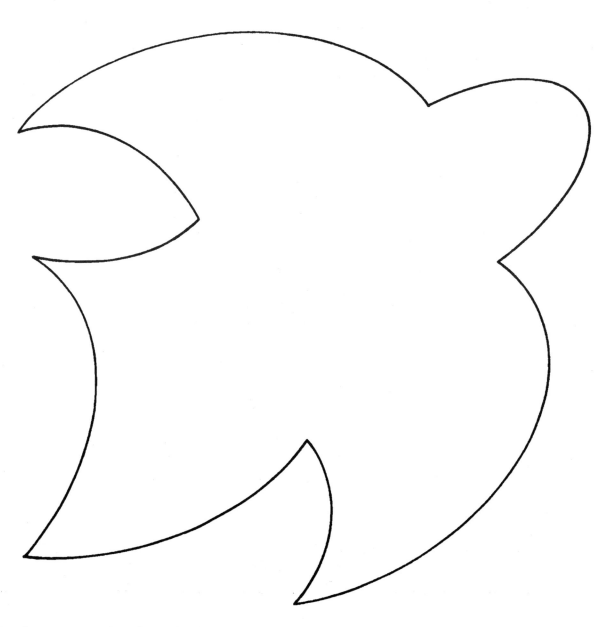

Vocal Prayer

Our voice is a gift from God. We can use it in prayer. We can say our prayers or we can sing them. We can say our prayers alone or with others. God hears each of us when we pray, no matter what voice we use.

Take the Chat Challenge

1. Poke a hole in the bottoms of two yogurt cups.
2. Thread 8 feet of string through each hole starting from the outside and tying your knot on the inside. Make sure your knot is large enough so it doesn't slip through when you pull the string tight.
3. Take the Chat Challenge and see if you and a friend can carry on a chat by talking into the cups. Note: Make sure the string is tight between the two of you.

Can you hear your friends 8 feet away if they are talking in a soft voice?

Make the connection! Pray.
Trace the line to connect the cups.

Our Prayer Light

Sitting quietly with Jesus is how two different kinds of prayers begin. For meditative and contemplative prayers, we pray quietly. We let our minds enjoy and fill with a sense of wonder for God.

Some people read the Bible and quietly let their minds focus on the words. Some people focus on a part of God's creation. Quietly they reflect on our amazing Father.

Color and cut out the pieces of the candle. Glue them in place to make a symbol of our light when we quietly think about God's wonders. An example of the finished candle is shown below.

How to Write a Prayer

Have you ever wondered how you might write a special prayer of your own? Each prayer has four parts. The first letter of each part spells the word ACTS.

Adoration

> We praise God.

Contrition

> We tell Him that we are sorry for any deeds that displease Him.

Thanksgiving

> We thank God for the many blessings He gives us.

Supplication

> Humbly ask God to hear our prayers and to give us what we ask for.

Write your own prayer using the ACTS above.

A _____

_____

C _____

_____

T _____

_____

S _____

_____

Basketful of Blessings

God created all good things. It is through Him that all those good things come. To receive God's good things is a blessing. When we bless another person or people in God's name, we are asking God to provide His divine help for them.

Make the box following the instructions and then fill it with slips of paper that list your many blessings.

handle →

basket
↓

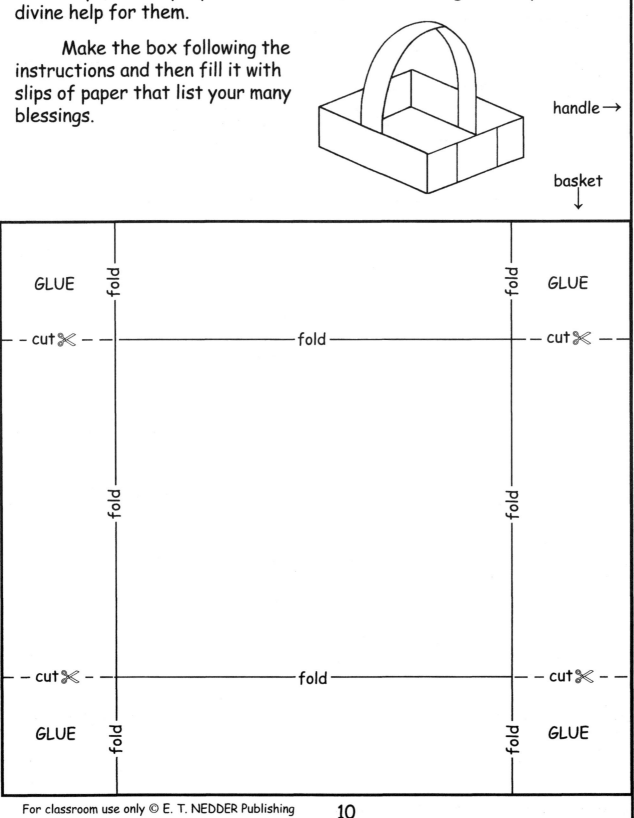

GLUE   fold   fold   GLUE

-- cut ✂ -- --------- fold --------- -- cut ✂ --

fold   fold

-- cut ✂ -- --------- fold --------- -- cut ✂ --

GLUE   fold   fold   GLUE

Petitions

When you ask for something, you are making a petition. We use petitions during the Mass just before the Offertory.

We also make petitions in informal prayer when we ask God to help us or others.

Write your own petitions, one on each strip. Cut on each line, and then make a chain with your petitions.

Dear God,

O Lord,

Dear God,

O Lord,

Dear God,

Cornucopia of Thanks

God the Father is the creator of Heaven and Earth. Everything that is, He created. In prayers of Thanksgiving, rejoice in the many wonders He gives us to enjoy.

A cornucopia symbolizes abundance and overflowing fullness. To make your Cornucopia of Thanks, roll a sheet of paper to make a large cone. Attach with glue or tape. Color and cut out pictures of things you are thankful for. Fill your cornucopia with them.

What do you enjoy?

Sun

Clothing

Nature   Food   Love

Father   Mother   Home

12

Trumpet God's Praises

Because God gives us all that is good, He deserves our love and praises. When we tell Him how amazing His creation is, we are praising God. When we tell Him how much we love the people in our lives, we are praising God.

1. Cut out the circle and its middle as indicated.
2. Roll the circle to line marks to make cone. Glue or tape in place.
3. Fold a sheet of 8½"x11" paper in half the long way. Cut on fold line.
4. Roll one of the rectangles to make a long tube that fits snugly inside the cone's circle. Glue or tape in place.
5. Cut out praise banner to hang on trumpet with yarn or string. Drape with colorful ribbons or string, then sing God's praises!

Pray with good
Reason
Alleluia
In every
Season on
Earth

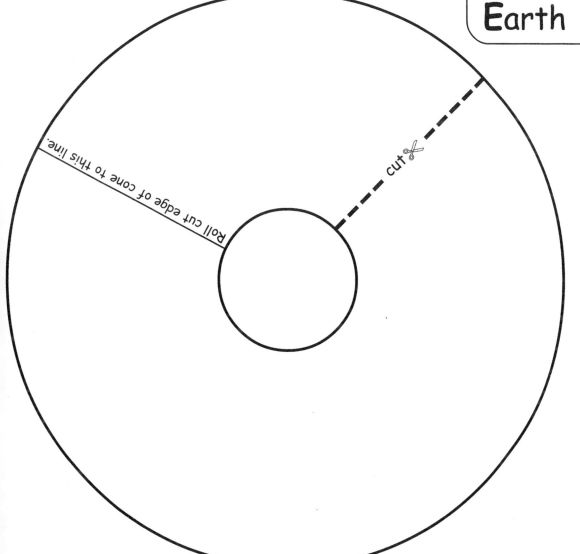

Roll cut edge of cone to this line.

cut

Intercession Session

Sometimes we pray to the holy people who live in Heaven. When we pray to them, we ask that they take our prayers to our Father in Heaven. We believe that they will take our requests to God, and because of their holy lives, God will give us what we ask for.

You know Jesus and Mary. How many saints do you know?

Make your own holy cards by drawing a picture of a saint in each box. Cut on the lines and write the saint's name on the back of each card.

Our Beliefs

The Apostles' Creed is a prayer that expresses all of the Catholic Church's major beliefs to share with its apostles. We are all apostles. We share these beliefs with every other Catholic from around the world.

Fill in the blanks with the appropriate words, then locate those words in the word find puzzle.

I believe in God, the _ _ _ _ _ _ Almighty, _ _ _ _ _ _ _ of _ _ _ _ _ _ _ and _ _ _ _ _; and in Jesus Christ, His only _ _ _, our Lord; Who was conceived by the Holy Spirit, born of the Virgin_ _ _ _, _ _ _ _ _ _ _ _ _ under Pontius Pilate, was_ _ _ _ _ _ _ _ _, died, and was buried. He descended into Hell; the _ _ _ _ _ day, He _ _ _ _ from the dead; He _ _ _ _ _ _ _ _ into Heaven, and sits at the _ _ _ _ _ hand of God, the Father _ _ _ _ _ _ _ _; He shall come to judge the _ _ _ _ _ _ and the _ _ _ _. I believe in the _ _ _ _ _ _ _ _ _ _, the Holy _ _ _ _ _ _ _ _ Church, the _ _ _ _ _ _ _ _ _ _ of Saints, the forgiveness of sins, the _ _ _ _ _ _ _ _ _ _ _ _ of the body, and life _ _ _ _ _ _ _ _ _ _ _ _. Amen.

```
C O M M U N I O N H T H I R D
F R A T H E R H T Y E A R T D
P C R E A T O R P A R G B S E
C S Y Q S N I V I L B N O S A
A R O S E A L M R M O I T U D
T I U W O M G E H I P T S F B
H G A C U N H R T G R S E F T
O E V W I T T C R H E A V E N
L A C H A F E B U T I L O R M
I R E F S R I G H Y T R N E I
C T E A R T P E A V N E M D H
H H N U F F E R D L I V I N G
U L S E T O R B U N I E H A T
T E R A S C E N D E D A E B Y
R I G H T H O L Y S P I R I T
```

The Communion of Saints

The Communion of Saints is the universal Church. All those who have died living in faith and all those living in faith are a part of the Communion of Saints.

That includes you! Your unique gifts and talents are so important to make the Communion of Saints complete. Every good action you do builds the Church and makes the Communion of Saints complete.

Each student should bring ½ cup of one of the following:

M & M's
Chocolate Chips
Raisins
Peanuts
Cereal
Pretzels
Mini-Graham Crackers

One at a time, combine all ingredients in a large bowl. Discuss how each contribution is tasty alone. How does the flavor change when each new ingredient is added to the mix?

Each of us is a gift by ourselves, but together with Christ as our leader, we are an amazing Communion of Saints!

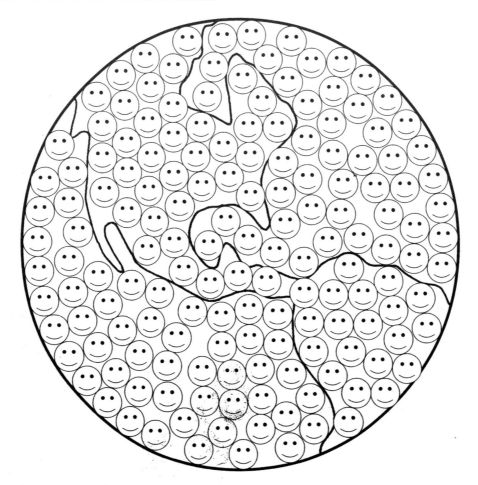

Color each face and see how the big picture changes into a work of art.

A Story of Stories

Make your own book using the words from the Apostles' Creed.

Instructions:

1. Fold three sheets of 8½" x 11" paper in half the short way.
2. Using the key, write the parts of the Creed on each sheet of folded paper.

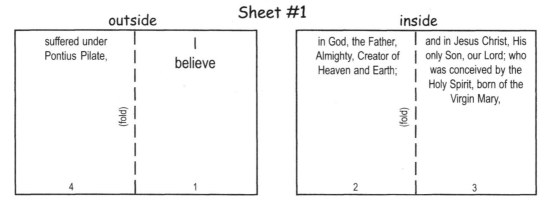

Sheet #1

outside

suffered under Pontius Pilate,	(fold)	I believe
4		1

inside

in God, the Father, Almighty, Creator of Heaven and Earth;	(fold)	and in Jesus Christ, His only Son, our Lord; who was conceived by the Holy Spirit, born of the Virgin Mary,
2		3

Sheet #2

outside

I believe in the Holy Spirit,	(fold)	was crucified, died, and was buried. He descended into Hell;
8		5

inside

the third day He rose from the dead; He ascended into Heaven,	(fold)	and sits at the right hand of God, the Father Almighty; He shall come to judge the living and the dead.
6		7

Sheet #3

outside

the resurrection of the body and life everlasting.	(fold)	the Holy Catholic Church,
12		9

inside

the Communion of Saints,	(fold)	the forgiveness of sins,
10		11

3. Then using crayons, markers or colored pencils, illustrate each page of your Story of Stories, the Apostles' Creed.
4. Finish your book by either stapling or punching two holes along the folded side and tying with yarn or string.

Bouquet of Grace

*Hail Mary, full of grace, the Lord is with you.
Blessed are you among women, and blessed is the
fruit of your womb, Jesus.*
*Holy Mary, mother of God, pray for us sinners,
now and at the hour of our death. Amen.*

We say Mary, full of grace, because she did what God
asked of her. God asks each of us to love Him and each other. We
show our love whenever we do good things for others. This shows our love
to others and to God because God lives in every person.

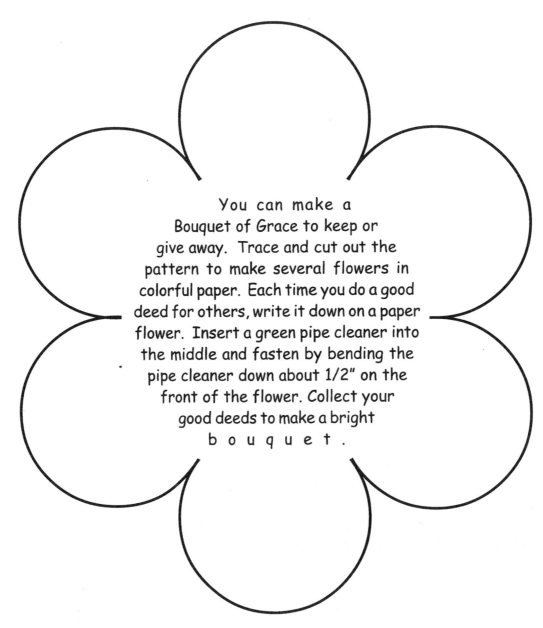

You can make a
Bouquet of Grace to keep or
give away. Trace and cut out the
pattern to make several flowers in
colorful paper. Each time you do a good
deed for others, write it down on a paper
flower. Insert a green pipe cleaner into
the middle and fasten by bending the
pipe cleaner down about 1/2" on the
front of the flower. Collect your
good deeds to make a bright
b o u q u e t .

18

Our Heavenly Mother

Mary is our heavenly mother. Just like our moms, she wants to help us get back to heaven.

The Hail Mary is a special prayer that praises Mary and Jesus and asks for Mary to pray for us now and at the hour of our death.

Which picture goes with each line taken from the Hail Mary?
Write the correct number in the correct circle.

1. Hail Mary, full of grace, the Lord is with you

2. Blessed is the fruit of your womb

3. Pray for us sinners

A Promise Full of Hope

The prayer, the Glory Be, promises us that God the Father, Son and Holy Spirit will always be with us, forever and ever.

Glory be to the _____ _,

and to the ___ ___ ___, and to the

_____ _____.

As it was in the

_____, is now and ever

shall be _____ without end.

Amen.

Glory Be - Three in One!

In the prayer, The Glory Be, we praise God the Father, Son and Holy Spirit – the Holy Trinity. One of their symbols is the triangle.

As you say this prayer, you see another triangle; the beginning, now and forever.

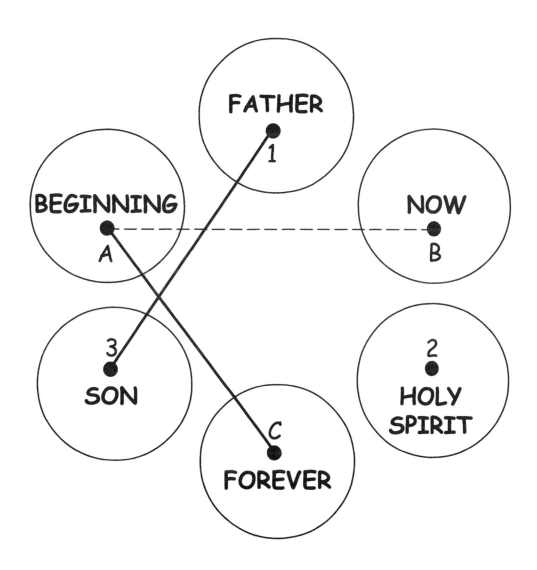

Connect the dots to make two triangles in the puzzle above. You will find another symbol for God's people!

Our Daily Bread

Our Father is the creator of all good things. We pray, "give us this day our daily bread." We are asking God to look after our needs.

Some of our needs are spiritual. He gives us the sacraments and the Eucharist.

Some of our needs are physical. For those, He gives us food and shelter.

You can share the Father's gift of daily bread with others when you make the bread below.

Pumpkin Bread

3 Cups White Sugar
3/4 Cup Vegetable Oil
3 Eggs
1-16 oz, Can Pumpkin
2/3 Cup Water
3 1/4 Cups Flour
2 Tsp. Baking Soda
1 Tsp. Salt

1. Combine sugar, oil, eggs, and pumpkin in large mixing bowl. Using mixer, beat well.
2. Add rest of ingredients to mixture in bowl. Mix till all ingredients are combined.
3. Grease two 9x5 loaf pans. Pour batter into pans.
4. Bake at 350 degrees for 1-1/2 hours, or until toothpick inserted in center of loaf comes out dry.
5. Cool for 10 minutes, then remove from pans and finish cooling on wire rack.

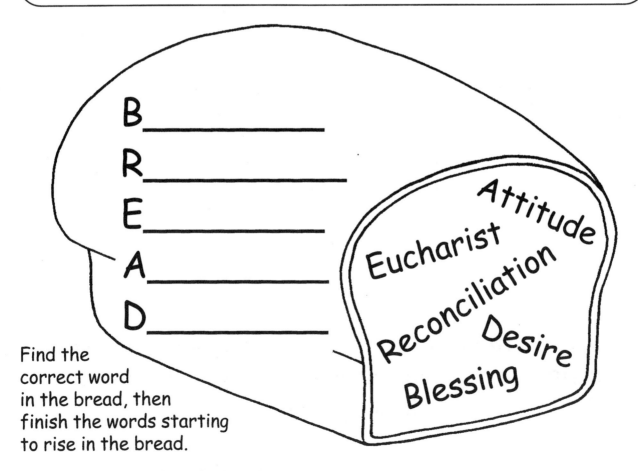

B _____
R _____
E _____
A _____
D _____

Eucharist
Attitude
Reconciliation
Desire
Blessing

Find the correct word in the bread, then finish the words starting to rise in the bread.

Our Father Rebus Activity

Jesus told us to call God, our Father. Use the clues to write the words and finish the prayer He gave us.

Our _____, who art in

_____, hallowed be thy name.

Thy kingdom come, Thy will

be done on _____ as it is in

_____. Give us this _____,

our daily _____, and _____ us

our _____, as we _____

those who _____ against us.

And lead us not into _____, but

_____ us from evil. Amen.

Morning Offering Mobile

The Morning Offering is a prayer that says we will live our whole day for Christ and His people. The Morning Offering Mobile is a fun way to remember to go through our day for Christ.

1. Cut out the shapes.
2. Color them with crayons, markers or colored pencils.
3. Poke a small hole through each piece as shown on the pattern.
4. Connect the mobile pieces as shown with four 7" pieces of string or yarn.
5. Tie a 7" piece of string or yarn through top of sun to hang.

Top

JOYS

24

The Morning Offering

O _____ through the Immaculate _____ of _____,

I offer you all of my _____, works, _____ and sufferings of this _____ with _____. For all of the intentions of your sacred heart, in _____ throughout the _____, in the Holy Sacrifice of the _____ throughout the _____, in reparation for my sins, but most of all for the _____ recommended this month by our Holy _____. Amen.

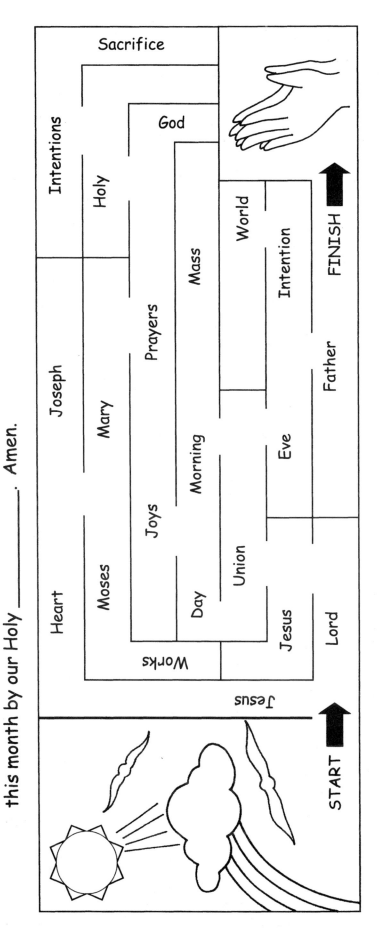

"I'm Sorry."

O my God, I am very sorry for offending you, and I detest all of my sins because they displease you who are all good and deserving of my love. I firmly resolve with the help of your grace to confess my sins, to do penance and to change my life. Amen.

The Act of Contrition is a way for us to tell God how sorry we are for our sins. Sometimes we hurt others by our words or actions. We feel better when we say we are sorry. Think of something for which you are sorry.

Using the card below, write a special note that tells how you feel.

(Illustrate front cover)

Dear _____,

_____

_____

_____

_____

_____

_____

_____.

_____

_____

The Act of Contrition

Use the puzzle code to discover what gift God gives us when we
say the Act of Contrition and receive the Sacrament of Reconciliation.

L – purple   O – orange   V – yellow   E – Green

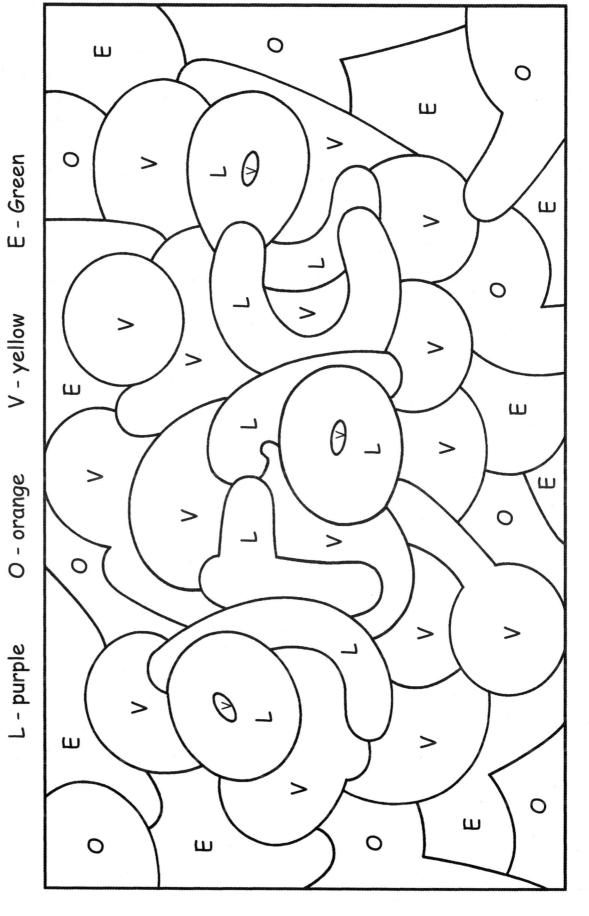

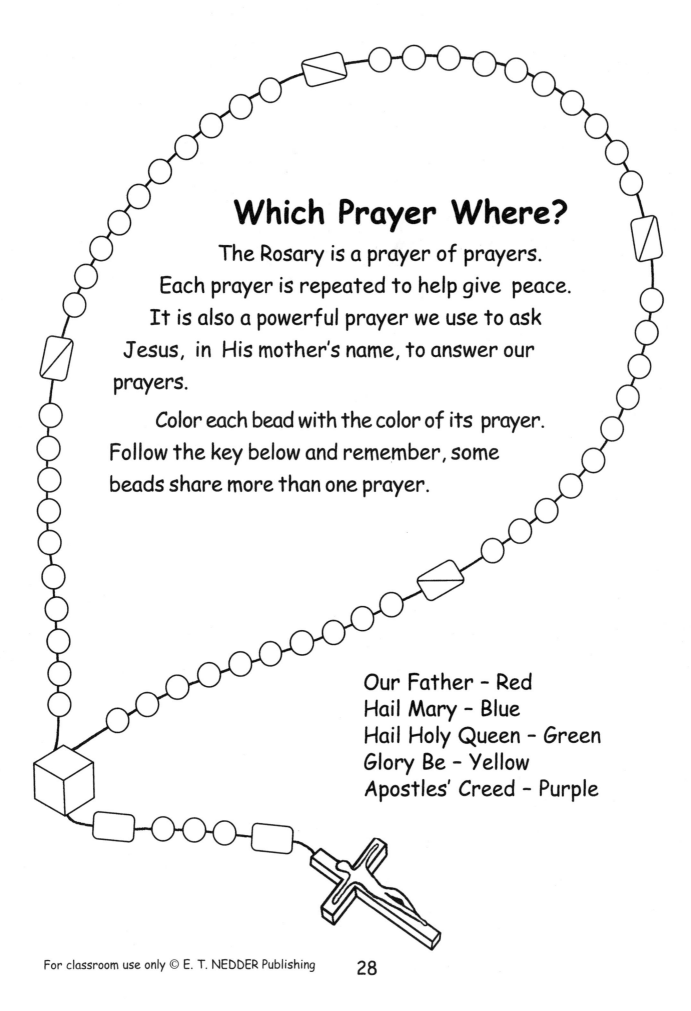

Which Prayer Where?

The Rosary is a prayer of prayers.
Each prayer is repeated to help give peace.
It is also a powerful prayer we use to ask
Jesus, in His mother's name, to answer our
prayers.

Color each bead with the color of its prayer.
Follow the key below and remember, some
beads share more than one prayer.

Our Father – Red
Hail Mary – Blue
Hail Holy Queen – Green
Glory Be – Yellow
Apostles' Creed – Purple

Hail Holy Queen, Mother of mercy, our life, our sweetness, and our
hope, to you do we cry poor banished children of Eve. To you do we send up
our sighs mourning and weeping in this valley of tears. Turn then most gracious
advocate, your eyes of mercy toward us, and after this our exile, show
unto us the blessed fruit of your womb, Jesus. O clement, O loving,
O sweet Virgin Mary. Pray for us, O Holy Mother of God, that
we may be made worthy of the promises of Christ.
Amen.

cut ✂

Crown fit for our Holy Queen

Instructions:

1. Cut along the dotted line at the top of the paper.
2. Pick one of the words from the prayer, Hail Holy Queen, and illustrate
it on the back side of this page using crayons, colored pencils or markers. Keep your art
between the two fold marks.

3. Connect several pages at fold using glue or tape

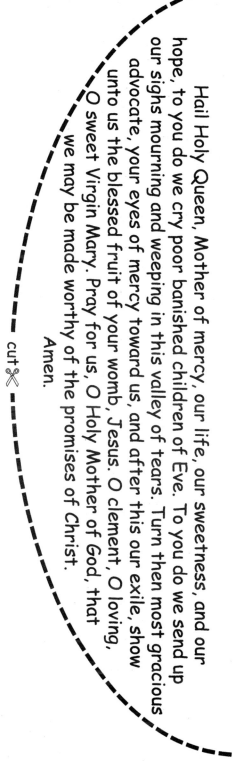

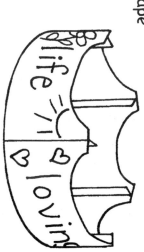

The Joyful Mysteries

The Joyful Mysteries are listed below, but some of the words are missing. Unscramble the word under each to complete the mystery.

1. The _____.
   NTICIONNUANA

2. The _____ of _____ to Elizabeth.
   ITATVIOSNI   RAMY

3. The _____.
   YTAVITIN

4. The _____ of the _____.
   IONTATNESEPR   SUJSE

5. The _____ of Jesus in the _____.
   GNIFNDI   EMLPET

The Sorrowful Mysteries

The Sorrowful Mysteries are in the wrong order. Follow the illustrations in the dot-to-dot below to help you find the correct order, then put the correct number 1-5 in front of each mystery.

___ The Scourging at the Pillar
___ The Agony in the Garden
___ The Crucifixion and Death of Jesus Christ
___ The Crowning with Thorns
___ The Carrying of the Cross

The Glorious Mysteries

This crossword puzzle reveals some wonderful news. Use the word list below to solve the puzzle and complete the listing of the Glorious Mysteries.

DESCENT

CORONATION

QUEEN

APOSTLES

ASCENSION

RESURRECTION

VIRGIN

HEAVEN

ASSUMPTION

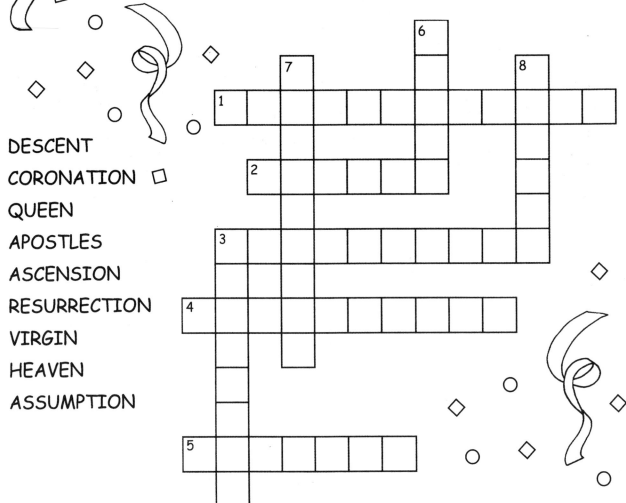

1. The _____ of Jesus from the dead.
   (1 – Across)

2. The _____ of Jesus into Heaven.
   (7 – Down)

3. The _____ of the Holy Spirit upon the _____.
   (5 – Across)   (3 – Down)

4. The _____ of the Blessed _____ Mary into Heaven.
   (3 – Across)   (8 – Down)

5. The _____ of Mary _____ of _____ and earth.
   (4 – Across)   (6 – Down)   (2 – Across)